Intel Embedded, and the Arduino-101

Patrick H. Stakem

Number 17 in the
Computer Architecture Series

(c) 2017

Introduction

This book follows Intel's excursions into the embedded space, with 8-, 16-, and 32-bit processors, derived from their general purpose computer line. Intel has traditionally dominated the desktop, laptop, and server market, but has increasingly addressed the embedded space, and the Internet of Things We take a look at Intel's licensing of the ARM architecture, and the contributions to that area. This leads to the latest development, an Arduino architecture that doesn't use a ARM chip, but rather an x86 chip. Of course, it executes a different set of opcodes, but the magic is, at the source level, it uses the same code as the Arm. We just need a new set of software tools. The Arduino-101 from Intel, an x-86 architecture internally, can run source code developed for the standard ARM-based Arduinos.

Author

Mr. Patrick H. Stakem received a Bachelors degree in Electrical Engineering from Carnegie-Mellon University, and Masters Degrees in Physics and Computer Science from the Johns Hopkins University.

He began his career in Aerospace with Fairchild Industries on the ATS-6 (Applications Technology Satellite-6), program, a communication satellite that developed much of the technology for the TDRSS (Tracking and Data Relay Satellite System). At Fairchild, Mr. Stakem made the amazing discovery that computers were put on board the spacecraft. He quickly made himself the expert on their support. He followed the ATS-6 Program through its operation phase, and worked on other projects at NASA's Goddard Space Flight Center including the Hubble Space Telescope, the International Ultraviolet Explorer (IUE), the Solar Maximum Mission (SMM), some of the Landsat missions, and others. He was posted to NASA's Jet Propulsion Laboratory for the MARS-Jupiter-Saturn (MJS-77), which later became the Voyager mission, which is still operating and returning data from outside the solar system at this writing.

Mr. Stakem was affiliated with the the Whiting School of Engineering of the Johns Hopkins University, the Graduate Computer Science Department of Loyola University in Maryland, and Capitol Technology University. He received NASA's Space Shuttle Program Managers commendation award.

Desktop/Server versus Embedded

Embedded refers to special purpose computers that are a part of a larger system, as opposed to generic desktop computers, tablets, and servers. Embedded systems are for specific purposes; they are not necessarily general purpose. They may have a limited or no human interface, but usually support complex I/O. The embedded computer can be characterized by the parameters of its central processing unit (CPU), memory, and input/output (I/O). The CPU parameters of importance are speed, power consumption, and price. The memory parameters include power consumption, speed, volatility, and size or capacity. I/O characteristics must be matched to external systems components.

Most microprocessors sold, by volume, are destined for embedded applications. They are purpose-built, and self-contained. Many include the features of BIST – built-in self-test.

Embedded systems can be found in most consumer products. Embedded systems, as opposed to traditional general-purpose desktop computers or tablets, are targeted toward a specific application or market, have specialized I/O, and limited user interfaces. You are, at the moment, surrounded by many embedded systems – your cell phone tv, washer, dryer, car, etc.

Although not a requirement, embedded computer systems are usually constructed from monolithic microprocessor chips. Previous generations have involved minicomputers. The air traffic control system is a large dedicated embedded system based on mainframes. Modern embedded systems might be Field Programmable Gate Array (FPGA)-based, or use a custom Application Specific Integrated Circuit (ASIC). Commodity pc boards can also form the basis of embedded system. It's just that Embedded systems don't usually need or can take advantage of all the bells and whistles included with low-cost, mass-manufactured desktop computer boards.

Embedded systems can be found everywhere: refrigerators, elevators, toothbrushes, vacuum cleaners, smartphones, automobiles, aircraft, running shoes, sewing machines, pacemakers, and more. There are a lot more embedded computers than general-purpose desktop, tablet, and server pc's. They are just sometimes harder to find.

System, as I use the word here, refers to the computer, memory, input-output, and the associated devices that the embedded computer controls or communicates with.

Embedded systems weren't always based on microprocessors. The first embedded systems were large mainframes, but evolved to minicomputers, and then microcomputers, when these became available. The first embedded system may have been the IBM Whirlwind computer in the 1940's which was designed to be real-time. Multicore single chip solutions are now the norm. This combines the central processing units, the memory, and the input-output on a single chip. This has the advantage of simplifying the circuit board design, minimizing the size, power consumption, and heat generation.

A microprocessor has come to mean a monolithic CPU, wholly contained on a single chip. Embedded microprocessors usually include memory and input-output circuitry as well. The first microprocessors were designed for calculators. They were 4-bit units that handled binary-coded decimal (bcd) digits, and did serial-by-digit calculations. They did it fast! In fact, the result appeared almost instantaneously to our eyes, unless you asked for something really hard, like 70-factorial. Then the calculator blinked. Texas Instruments and Hewlett-Packard repeatedly outdid each other in producing hand-held calculators with more functionality and less cost. But the 4-bit chips evolved into 8-bit models, and were made more general purpose.

Automobiles have used microprocessor-based controllers since the 1970's. There was a desire to reduce emissions, and simultaneously increase both fuel economy and performance. This was not going to happen with mechanical systems such as carburetors. Analog controllers were tried, but were troublesome. Then, 8-bit, and later 16-bit embedded processors used look-up tables in memory to determine the exact optimal operating time for the fuel injectors, based on multiple input parameters from engine sensors. 32-bit processors allowed for the function to be calculated in real-time, and the look-up table was no longer required.

32-bit processors could also do the required calculations for anti-lock brakes. With anti-lock brakes, you can get traction control and stability control almost for free.

The trend now is to include more than one CPU on the chip, called Multicore technology. In addition, specialized processor units for floating point, vector processing, and digital signal processing are included. Multicore changes the game.

Many embedded systems are required to be real-time - they have strict deadlines. Others are event-driven - a trigger event kicks off a predetermined sequence of responses. Embedded systems are almost always resource constrained. The resources might be size, weight, power, throughput, heat generation, reliability, deadlines, etc. Embedded systems have a high non-recurring engineering (NRE) cost (development cost), but are generally cheap to produce in volume. Embedded computers rarely host their own development system.

Although the thrust of early Reduced Instruction Set Computing (RISC) development was enhanced computation that usually found itself in engineering workstations, the market for such endeavors was limited in scope. A much larger market, and, more importantly, a volume market, was found in embedded control. Volume markets are cost driven. Now, most computer architecture is RISC.

An important concept emerges here: although we usually associate RISC with 32- or even 64-bit machines, this is not necessarily always true. For a counterexample, consider the Microchip PIC, which represents a minimalist 8-bit approach to RISC for embedded control. More importantly, conventional RISC manufacturers, who might produce 50-100,000 units for the workstation market, are finding the multi-billion piece embedded systems market appealing. This is a production environment, with the customer hand-holding done once, at development time. After that, the process involves turning out product and shipping it. Volume embedded control markets include laser printers, fax machines, cellular communication devices, set-top boxes, sewing machines, large appliances, keyless entry systems, etc. Emerging markets are automotive engine and transmission controls, smart appliances, smart cars, high-end video games, and more. These devices have created a market larger than any traditionally known.

In automotive applications of embedded systems, the market has exploded. This includes sensors, memory, and device control. Embedded automotive processors can be found in airbag/crash systems, roll-over and stability control, engine control and monitoring, transmission control and monitoring, *infotainment* systems, driver assist systems, and systems monitoring and management. Hybrid (gas-electric) and full eklectric vehicles feature advanced battery management, "fuel state" calculation, and powertrain control.

Some of the parameters of importance in embedded computing include interrupt latency, integrated solutions for low chip count, and good development tools for quick time to market. The processor is usually characterized by its word size (number of bits), its clock speed, and its instruction set.

The advantage of using a commodity mass-produced platform is that it is readily available and cheap. At the same time, it may need additional hardware resources, and it may not be well adapted to real-time operations. The use of industry standard interfaces such as USB further reduces costs and simplifies the design. The real-time issues may be addressed by the proper choice of operating system.

Early products

We should mention that an embedded system can be built with the same processors designed for the desktop, but special embedded models will include more resources to address the embedded domain, and allow for lower power and lower chip count.

Intel started out in the microprocessor world with a 2-bit ALU, the I-3002. This was a bit-slice processor, so you could string 4 of these together to get an 8-bit unit. The 2001 unit was the controller for these. This reflects the limitations of the manufacturing technology of the time. Later, the monolithic 4004 and 4040 models, 4-bit processors, were developed for adding machines, which can use the BCD number format, and serial-by-digit computation. Beats a slide rule, trust me.

Intel continued development, and came out with the 8008 8-bit processor with a 16 bit address. It went into production in 1972. It was developed specifically for a customer, Control Terminal Corporation, for their desk top calculator, the Datapoint 2200. The chip had 3,500 transistors in a PMOS technology, with 10 micron line width. There were 48 instructions. The address space was 16 kilobytes, but direct addressing was not supported. The H and L registers had to be loaded with the memory address. The 8008 required a complex clock, and significant amounts of external logic

8-bit

The 8080 was a great improvement over the prior 8008 chip, incorporating many features into the chip that required external hardware with the 8008. It could be considered a superset of the 8008 design. The 8080 was an NMOS chip, with 8-bit words and a 16-bit address bus. It required plus and minus 5 volts and plus 12 volts. It drew 0.8 watts. The circa-1973 chip was a sequential state machine design, where the current state is a function of the previous state, and current inputs. It used 6,000 transistors, and operated at 2 MHz (later, 3 MHz). It was designed by Federico Faggin, and released in 1974. It had 48 instructions, and was a general purpose processor.

The Intel approach to Input-Output is to use a separate I/O address space and specific I/O instructions. This does not preclude using memory-mapped I/O. The 8080 had 256 inputs and 256 outputs, each one byte wide. (Thus, the I/O address was 8 bits). The Accumulator register held the I/O address.

A follow-on product, the 8085, was an improvement to the 8080, but still was intended as a general purpose part. It did bring a lot of support functions onboard the chip, which previously needed separate chips. A

12

separate chip, the 8231, provided hardware multiple and divide. The 8085 was not intended as an embedded controller, but found application in that area. The 8085 was used in several space missions, including NASA's OSS series spacecraft. It was also used on the 1997 JPL Mars Pathfinder Rover Sojourner. The attitude control system on NASA's WIRE spacecraft used an 80C85, as did the FAST and XTE missions.

The 8048, in 1976, was designed to be a microcontroller, with data storage on-chip. It had single byte instructions, stored in external ROM. It included 64 bytes of RAM, and 27 I/O lines. Later versions had 1k or 4k of internal ROM. The 8049 model had two timers, and the 8050 had four times the RAM and ROM. The 8748 and 49 had EPROM in place of ROM, so they could be programmed by the customer. These chips eventually ran at 6-11 MHz, and were available in CMOS technology for low power.

The 8051 was developed from the earlier 8048 as an embedded control processor by Intel in 1980. The 8048 had serial I/O plus dual timers, 4k of ROM, and 128 bytes of RAM. They operated up to 16 MHz, and came in ROM-less versions (8031), and in CMOS. The 8044 was an 8051 with a synchronous serial interface to a host machine, and EPROM.

The Intel 8051 was developed from the 8048 as an embedded control processor by Intel in 1980. Embedded processors can operate with fewer external parts, and the 8051 includes memory and Input/Output on the same chip. They had serial I/O plus dual timers, 4k of ROM, and 128 bytes of RAM. They operated up to 16 MHz, and came in ROM-less versions (8031), and in CMOS. The 8044 was an 8051 with a synchronous serial interface to a host machine, and EPROM.

The 8742 was an associated peripheral 8-bit slave microcontroller, meant to be used with the 8051, 8048, and even the general purpose 8080 and 8085. It was a follow-on to the 8741 with twice the memory. It was a peripheral chip, but included a complete 8-bit cpu, with 2k of EPROM, 128 bytes of RAM, a clock/timer, and I/O control lines. It was intended to offload I/O from the main cpu. (let me date myself here – like an IBM Mainframe channel processor). It supported asynchronous transfer with the main processor.

Many manufacturers still offer versions of the 8051, and it is widely used in college-level embedded systems courses. The most recent instantiations of the design include IP (intellectual property) core versions, for implementation within FPGA's that need one or more CPU's. Why re-invent the wheel, when the 8051 comes with a development history, loyal following, and support tools? The 8051 was used on NASA's environmental satellites Aqua and Aura.

16-bit

The 80186 was an embedded version of the general purpose 8086, incorporating an integral clock generator, dual dma channels, interrupt controllers, and chip selects. This greatly reduced the number of external chips required in a design. It could address 64k of 8-bit I/O ports, or 32k of 16-bit ports, and supported 256 vectored interrupts. The 186 had roughly twice the performance of the 8086. The 80188 was a 80186, with an 8-bit external bus. This allows for the use of less expensive 8-bit wide memory, at the cost of access time. Each memory word access (16-bits) required two 8-bit wide sequential memory accesses. The 186 and 188 included some additional devices on the same chip, to reduce chip count in a system, while maintaining compatibility with the ISA-86.

The Intel MCS-96 family of embedded microcontrollers was derived from the 8061 chip. It resulted from a project for the Ford Motor Company, for a 16-bit engine controller. This unit was called the EEC-IV. The 8061 had 8 pulse measuring inputs, 10 pulse generating outputs, and multichannel 10-bit A/D. Later variants included onchip ram and rom.

The 809x parts operated at 12 MHz. They included a CPU, a 4-channel, 10-bit A/D, a 8-bit PWM, a watch-dog timer, and four general 16-bit timers. They featured hardware multiply and divide, and 8 kbytes of ROM. The 8095 version came with no internal ROM, but did include high speed I/O plus a serial port. CMOS versions of the chip were available.

32-bit

The 80376 was an embedded variation of 386 architecture introduced in 1989. It did not support Intel's real mode, but booted directly to protected mode. It was replaced by the 80386EX, which was a static design, true 32-bit processor with extensive peripherals on chip. It included power management circuitry, up to 24 I/O lines, 3 channels of 8254- equivalent timer/counters, two 8259-equivalent interrupts controllers, dual full-duplex Async serial (uart) channels, one synchronous five mbps I/O channel with baud rate generator, DRAM refresh, 32-bit watchdog timer, dual channel DMA control, and JTAG debugging support. The 16-bit bus variations of Intel's 32-bit general purpose architectures, the i386sx and i484sx, found application in embedded as well. The UoSat project used the 80386sx.

The Intel i960 was a 32-bit RISC embedded processor family dating from 1984. They were not code-compatible with other Intel products. They featured 32, 32-bit registers, with a priority interrupt controller, on-chip instruction cache (1k to 16k), with data cache (1k to 8k) on some models, a PCI controller, and a memory controller on chip. Some models included dual 32-bit timers and an i2c bus. They were a superscalar architecture with register scoreboarding. Some models also had an integral IEEE-754 floating point unit.

The processor is still in use. It's design was influenced by the iAPX432 project at Intel, and the i960 design was a joint effort with Siemens. In order not to compete with its own i860 and i386 products in the general purpose computing market, Intel targeted the i960 to the embedded market. The i960 followed the Berkeley school of RISC design, with register windows and fast subroutine calls. The memory space was flat.

Note: the Core i7 960 is an x86 architecture.

Atom

The Intel Atom cpu is a 32-bit x86 architecture optimized for low power. It was introduced in 2008, and is available in multicore and hyper-threaded editions, with speeds beyond 2 GHz. There are generally three models – N for low power, Z for mobile devices, and D for low-end desktop and D for low end laptop and desktop.It translates x86 instructions into internal RISC instructions on the fly, and can execute two integer instructions per clock. Because the parts are IA-32 and IA-64 compatible, there is a large amount of available legacy software available. System-on-a-chip devices based on the Atom were phased in, in 2012, targeting the IoT market. The SoC devices were built in a partnership with Google, and were meant to run the Android operating system for phones and tablets. The Atom was roughly comparable to an ARM Cortex-A8 in performance, but has a factor of 4 more power draw. The Atom features in-order instruction execution, and has branch prediction. It has a relatively slow divide. The SSE unit is faster in doing floating point calculations than the built-in floating point unit (x87). The Atom supports Intel's real and protected modes, as well as hyperthreading, where each physical processor core can support 2 logical cores. This technique increases the utilization of the execution unit, which can be both good and bad. They also have a Turbo Boost feature, where they can be overclocked for brief periods, limited by heat generation. This involves both clock rate and voltage. There is also hardware support for virtualization, and support for security with trusted execution. The x86 architecture scales, as we have seen from the original 8086 in 1978, to the latest Atom model. It also now supports 64 bits, as an architecture extension. The x86 processors use a version of the 8086-era 8259 Interrupt Controller. With the 8086, it was a separate chip. Now it is included with the cpu, but works the same. Interrupt vectors are kept in protected memory.

The Atom processor, E3900 series, and it's companion units, the Celeron-based N3350 and Pentium-based N4200 directly address the Internet of Things. All come in a quad-core configuration, and are implemented as a module (compact flipchip ball grid array). The N3350 operates up to 2.4 GHz. All of the models support up to 8 gigabytes of DRAM. The 4200 has a Pentium with a 2 megabyte cache, and operates up to 2.5 GHz. The Atom-based units have 2 megabytes of cache. The three units use an X-5 or an X-7 cpu.

Atom has some features targeted to the embedded world, such as Intel's Speedstep, which is a low power sleep mode. It does support JTAG. Ubuntu release a special version of its linux for Atom-based netbooks, called Ubuntu Netbook Remix.

The E3900 model can have a dual or quad core, with an associated image processor (the IMPU4), dma; SATA connections, 6 USB-3 and 2 USB-2, 3 SPI, 1-SDIO, and support for an SD card. The high performance graphics unit can have up to 18 execution units. There are dual audio DSP's, and it can interface up to four MIPI-CSI cameras. There are four PCI-express ports.

The Atom does in-order execution, 2 instructions per clock. It does support the CPUID instruction, introduced with the 80486. This instruction returns identification data on the cpu, as well as cpu features. Software can then tell what cpu version it is running on.

The Atom has on-chip instruction trace, via JTAG.

Virtualization

We should take a moment and look at virtualization, and the included hardware support. X86 virtualization allows for multiple x-86 operating systems to share base x86 resources simultaneously, and is an example of hardware virtualization.

A computer is a general-purpose machine with compute, memory and input/output resources. We can virtualize any or all of these resources.

Virtualization is an isomorphism from guest to host, if we want to get mathematical. We map the guest state to the host state, implement equivalent functions, and we get one machine pretending to be another, or a bunch of "others." The key is, if you can touch it, it is the physical machine, the host. Otherwise it is the guest. Just like a guest at a resort, you get access to the resources you've paid for, but not total access. That's reserved for management.

There are many ways to do this. We can have hardware virtualization, where the host machine acts like a real machine with a real operating system that is stand-alone. Most importantly, it can act like several real machines. We can run Linux on a Windows machine or Windows on a Linux machine, or a bunch of Windows machines on a single host.

We can have full virtualization, which is a complete or nearly complete simulation of the existing hardware. This allows the guest operating system and its applications to run unmodified.

We can also have partial virtualization, where some but not all of the host are available. The guest operating system and the applications may need to be modified.

In paravirtualization, the hardware environment is not simulated, but the guests operating systems need to be aware of the hypervisor. They are slightly modified versions of the base operating system. Paravirtualized guests generally run faster because of the lack of the emulation layer.

Virtualization is hard, not just to implement but also to run. If it can get specific assistance from the platform hardware, it can run faster. This is the trend from the chip manufacturers; to add specific virtualization assistance in the chip design.

In Intel's defined Protected mode, the operating system kernel runs at a high privilege (ring 0) and applications at a low privilege level such as ring 3. One approach is to run the hypervisor at ring 0 privilege, and the operating system at a lower level. Certain operating system instructions require certain ring levels to be able to execute, however. Binary translation can be used to replace these with other instructions that will execute at a lower level. The process is called trap and emulate, but this involves overhead.

Hardware assist to virtualization, provided by Intel involves both the privileged instructions, and MMU support. These were implemented in different ways. Intel's initial hardware virtualization support, called "Vanderpool" was released on Pentium 4 models in 2005. I/O virtualization can be enabled in the BIOS.

Although virtualization was slow to be adopted in the embedded space, it is now seeing more use, as the chips have enough resources to support it. For IA-32 and -64, the feature is called VT-intel. It is VT-X in the Atom feature.

Protected mode

Protected Mode, introduced on the 32 bit architectures, is the key to memory management in IA-32. Because of the need at the time to support 16-bit legacy features on 32-bit hardware at the time, the implementation was complex.

Operating systems such as OS/2, UNIX, Linux, bsd, and Windows take advantage of Protected Mode's advanced features.

The 80386 and subsequent chips enter real mode at reset. This mode is comparable with 8086. By software, you can command an entry to protected mode.

In protected mode, there is a 16-bit segment selector plus a 16-bit offset to yield a 32-bit virtual address. The virtual address is what the running program uses. The system converts the virtual address to a physical address (in real time) that goes out over the memory bus to the system's memory. There is more virtual memory than real memory. The bookkeeping is handled by the system, partially in hardware and partially in software.

In protected mode, you have all the features of real mode, plus virtual addressing and layers of protection.

Virtual Addressing

The physical address space is what you have to work with. The virtual address space is what you pretend to have to work with. The processor does the dynamic mapping between virtual and physical address. This memory management technique is called address translation, and requires additional overhead on each memory access.

With virtual memory, you can write applications that assume you have 1 gigabyte available, and rely on the operating system to swap the correct virtual memory pages into and out of the existing physical memory. This, of course, takes time.

Virtual memory

We can use hard disk space used as memory, in the form of a swap file. Disk memory is much less expensive than semiconductor memory, but much slower as well. The virtual memory is mapped through regular memory. In additional to the penalty of the speed, there is extensive software overhead as well in the translation process. Thrashing refers to the scenario where the system is caught up in swapping memory, without getting anything else done.

In the Intel scheme, the high memory area is the first 64k of extended memory. Through a quirk of the addressing scheme, this can be addressed in real mode.

To understand the physical address calculation process in protected mode, we should first review the Physical Address Calculation in real mode. There is a 16-bit segment specifier plus a 16-bit offset. The address is in two 16-bit parts, a segment and an offset. We shift the segment part over to the left by four bits (or, equivalently, multiply it by 16), and add the offset. We get a 20-bit result.

Physical address = segment * 16 + offset

This provides a 20-bit physical address which spans 2^{20} = 1 megabyte of address space.

In protected mode, there is a 16-bit segment selector plus a 16-bit offset concatenated to yield a 32-bit virtual address. The virtual address is what the running program uses. The system converts the virtual address to a physical address (in real time) that goes out over the memory bus to the system's memory. There is more virtual memory than real memory. The bookkeeping is handled by the system, partially in hardware and partially in software.

Along with protected mode, Intel introduced the ring model of privilege, modeled on the earlier UNIX approach. There are 4 concentric layers, where the innermost is the most trusted, and the outermost is the user program. This model is in use to the present day. The innermost layer is now used for the Hypervisor, and the next layer down for the operating system. But, there are problems to this implementation that complicate it.

The base address of the segment in memory is not calculated by multiplying the segment specifier by 16, but rather by indexing a table in memory. This table, previously set up by the program or operating system, is called the descriptor table. It contains more than just the address translation information.

The Selector Table contains entries called selectors. Selectors contain three fields:

> The Requested Privilege Level (RPL),
> The Table Indicator (TI), and
> Index (I)

The RPL field does not concern address translation, but is used by the operating system to implement privilege level protection. It is a number 0-3. The intent is to prevent a less-privileged program from accessing data from a more privileged one.

The TI field specifies the table to be used by the Global Descriptor Table (TI = 0) or the Local Descriptor Table (TI = 1). These are data structures residing in memory, and set up by the operating system. The Global Descriptor Tables registers point to global Descriptor Tables. The Descriptor Table Registers can be read and written by specific instructions; the GDTR by the instructions LGDT and SGDT, and the LDTR by LLDT and SLDT.

The Index is a pointer into the table. Descriptors are 8 bytes long. The index item is a 24-bit address for the corresponding segment (on the 80286. 32-bits on 80386 and subsequent).

The 24-bit address obtained from the selector table look-up is added to the 16 bit offset to form a 24-bit physical address. Overflows are ignored, thus addresses wrap around.

If TI = 0 (GDT) and Index = 0, this is the null selector. If it is used for address translation, it results in an exception.

The index field is 13 bits, so a descriptor table can have up to 2^{13} descriptors. Each describes a segment of 2^{16} bytes. So, each task can have a private memory space of 2^{29} bytes. A segment is 64k bytes on the 80286. On the 80386 and subsequent, with 32-bit offset addresses, the virtual address space is 2^{46} bytes.

Segment descriptors are located in the descriptor table. They consist or two parts, a base address and a limit. They contain status and control information for access. They provide a link between a task, and a segment in memory.

Memory descriptors specify a type, code or data. Code is executable, data can be read-only or read-write. These

25

distinctions are imposed by the data structure; the memory is Von Neumann, and read-write. The Type field differs for code and data. The code segment can be accessed, can be readable or not, and is conforming or not. The data segment can be accessed, write-able or not, and expands up or expands down (like a stack).

The access byte contains an indicator bit about whether the segment is physically present in memory or not.

Another complication of protected mode includes the fact that the math coprocessor (x87) also has a protected mode, and interrupt servicing in Protected Mode involves an Interrupt descriptor table, interrupt gates, and call gates.

In protected mode, calling and jumping involve an inter-segment FAR call through a call gate. The privilege level of the caller is checked against the privilege of the called program (in the gate descriptor). It the level is not good enough, a general protection fault (INT 0D$_h$) is generated.

Before entering protected mode, all of the necessary data structures such as the descriptors tables, must be properly set up. This is an operating system function. Then the LMSW (load machine status word) instruction is executed, with the PE (protection enable) bit = 1. Simple, But.... First, the instruction queue must be flushed. This is because the instructions were fetched in real mode, but are executed in protected mode. How do we flush the queue? Simply do a short jump to the very next location beyond the jump. Jumps force an instruction queue flush. The astute reader will notice that the short jump is fetched in real mode and executed in protected mode, but that's ok – it works.

Return to real mode simply requires resetting the PE bit by instruction.

Another concept that came along with Protected Mode was that of tasks. There can be many tasks in the system, only one running at a time. These are controlled by the operating system (itself a task) with the TSS-Task State Segment structure. This contains the task state (essentially, register contents). The processor has a task register for the currently running task that is user-visible. There are also pointers (not visible) to the TSS. The Task register is loaded and stored with the LTR/STR instructions. The TSS descriptor looks like a descriptor that we have talked about, but has an idle/busy bit. Tasks are not re-entrant under this scheme.

The Task gate descriptor is an indirect, protected way of accessing a task. It resides in the GDT. A task that does not have enough privilege to use the TSS descriptor can call another task through a gate in the LDT.

Task switching is managed by the operating system, and involves controlled calls and jumps. Interrupts are also managed.

Virtual-86 mode was introduced in the 80386 as an 8086 emulation mode. The 80386 can implement multiple 8086 environments running "simultaneously" in protected environments. These are virtual machines.

There are some minor differences in how memory above 1 megabyte is treated.

.

Page level protection was implemented on the 80386 and subsequent processors. This involves a user/supervisor bit, and supervisor write protection. Paging uses smaller, fixed-size memory blocks. Segmentation uses larger, variable size blocks. Page mode is enabled with a single bit. It can be used with segmentation, as an additional layer of protection, with additional overhead. Pages in the x86 are 4096 bytes, at an address divisible by 1000_h. The page directory and tables are used to control the pages. CR3, the control register, has the page frame address or the page directory in the high order 20 bits. The page directory can hold 1 million entries. Each entry is a pointer to a page table. The page table contains pointers to physical memory.

MMX extensions, SSE

Intel x86 processors added a single-instruction multiple-data (SIMD) extension to the architecture called MMX, MultiMedia Extension, in 1997. It includes eight new 64-bit registers. These registers are meant to hold eight 8-bit integers, four 16-bit integers, or two 32-bit integers, which will be operated upon in parallel. After Intel received a license to build Arm processors, it added it's MMX architecture to the ARM world.

The MMX registers are actually mapped into the floating point registers, making it tricky to do floating point and MMX operations simultaneously. The floating point registers are 80 bits wide, and the MMX registers use the lower 64 bits. The MMX extension has continued in the IA-32 and IA-64, but more SIMD operations for graphics are now included. The XMM registers are used in SIMD calculations. They are 128-bits in size. The IA-32 architecture has 8, and the IA-64 has 16.

MMX supports saturation arithmetic. In this scheme, all operations are limited to a fixed range between a defined minimum and maximum. Values beyond those limits are not recognized. The mathematical properties of associativity and distributivity are not applicable in saturation arithmetic. An alternative to saturation arithmetic is where the values wrap-around, which unfortunately changes the sign in two's-complement representation. For audio processing (louder-than-loud) and video processing (blacker-than-black), saturation arithmetic works fine. It's the issue of getting an answer "close enough" in the time allowed. Saturation arithmetic plays an important role in digital signal processing techniques for video and audio processing.

SSE extensions

In 1999, Intel introduced the Streaming SIMD Extensions (SSE) architecture with the Pentium-III, and later the SSE2 with the Pentium 4. This has new 128-bit registers, and a corresponding instruction set extension. An SSE and a floating point instruction cannot be issued in the same cycle, due to onchip resource conflicts. SSE2 introduced double precision floating point support. SSE has 70 additional instructions to support operations for digital signal processing and graphics. SSE3 added new digital signal processing features, and

SSE4 added an instruction for vector dot product.

Advanced Vector Extensions (AVX) introduced a 256-bit data path, and 3-operand instructions. These are extensions to the x86 architecture. These units can operate on 256 or 512 bit data structures. AVX-2 extends integers to 256 bits, and adds bit manipulation and multiply. AVX-512 extends data and operations to 512 bits. Vector data can be loaded from non-contiguous memory locations, referred to as gather, and stored to non-contiguous locations, called scatter. Exponential and reciprocal instructions accelerate transcendental functions. They implement the fused multiply-add operation, which looks like: $X = \text{round}\ (a \times b + c)$.

Tolapi

This is an Intel system-on-a-chip, based on a Pentium M core, with included I/O and security. The current clock rates extend to 1.2 GHz. It has a 256k onchip cache, and supports DDR external ram. I/O and interfacing support includes a local expansion bus, PCI express, dual SATA, 1G Ethernet, dual CAN controllers, dual high speed serial interfaces, dual UARTs, and a LPC and SPI interfaces. There is real time clock support, and an enhanced DMA controller. These units support the instructions MMX, SSE, SSE2 and SSE3.

TSX-ni is an architectural extension to IA-86, the Transactional Synchronization Extensions. This supports transactional memory to simplify concurrent programming. Essentially, in transactional memory, a set of load or store instructions can be concurrent.

ARM embedded

The ARM processor has come a long way from being an obscure British microprocessor of the 1980's to being the dominant embedded architecture. They are used extensively in television set-top boxes, routers, and embedded applications. The ARM architecture parts still represent the highest volume of 32-bit processors being shipped, as of this writing.

In 2010, over 6 billion ARM chips were sold, mostly into the smartphone market. ARM is the target architecture for the GNU/linux-based Android operating system, and the ARM has ports of OpenSolaris, FreeBSD, OpenBSD, NetBSD, and various GNU/linux variations, including Gentoo, Debian, Slackware, and Ubuntu, among others.

In 1983, the British company Acorn Computers Ltd. was shopping for a new 16-bit processor to replace the 8-bit Mostek 6502 that they were then using. Some say that Acorn was rejected by Intel, others say that Acorn didn't like either the Intel 80286 or the Motorola MC 68000. In any case, the company decided to develop its own processor called the Acorn RISC Machine, or ARM. The company had been started in Cambridge, UK, in 1978. The name Acorn was supposed to suggest expandability and growth. The company had development samples, known as the ARM1, by 1985; production models (ARM2) were ready the following year. The original ARM chip contained 30,000 transistors. Acorn Computers was taken over by Olivetti in 1985 and renamed Element 14, LTD, in 1999 (element number 14 is silicon). That company was in turn taken over by Broadcom in the year 2000.

The ARM started out as destined for the desktop, but along the way, got diverted mostly to embedded use. Now, more powerful ARM chips are beginning to challenge the pc and server markets, currently owned by the Intel architecture.

ARM is an Instruction Set Architecture (ISA) specification. It is instantiated in silicon by numerous companies world-wide under license. ARM Holdings PLC, a British Multinational company, is the inheritor of the intellectual property (IP) of the 32-bit CPU design, and licenses its use worldwide. Derivative products include the Freescale series, the Xscale, Samsung's Hummingbird, the A4 and A5 by Apple, and Texas Instruments products incorporating digital signal processing functionality, among others. This is similar to the situation with Intel's ISA-32, with chips of that architecture built by Intel, and chips with a different implementation of the architecture built under license by AMD and others. The Intel ISA-16 and ISA-32 addressed the desktop and server market, but embedded versions were also available.

The ARM architecture today accounts for more than 75% of all 32-bit embedded processors. Hundreds of millions are in cellular phones and tablets. The ARM architecture provides a simple and standard platform for embedded systems. Embedded systems differ in their architecture and requirements from desktop and server architectures. The problem domains have different requirements. Where the Intel x86 architecture came to dominate the desktop and server areas, the ARM architecture dominates the small embedded market. A good hardware architecture definition is necessary, but it must be accompanied by an equally good software architecture. Code can be developed in Java or variants of c or other languages and many off-the-shelf operating systems are available. The ARM architecture reached critical mass in the embedded market niche. ARM separates the Intellectual Property of the design and the Instruction Set Architecture from the implementation. The ARM architecture has at this point more than 700 licenses, and it grows by 100 per year.

The Arduino architecture

The Arduino is an open source microcontroller produced by numerous company's. It can be 8 bits or 32 bits. Actually, the Arduino has become a concept, that many are building hardware to. The boards are built to one of several standard form factors, and are stackable with their families of various I/O There is a lot of commonality among boards, but they are seldom the same.

Arduino was born in 2005 at the Ivrea Interaction Design Institute in Italy as an easy tool for fast prototyping, aimed at students without a background in electronics and programming.

A typical Arduino board consists of an 8-bit Atmel AVR microcontroller or a 32-bit ARM. An important aspect of the Arduino is the standard way that connectors are arranged, allowing the CPU board to be connected to a variety of interchangeable add-on modules called *shields*. Shields allow for interfacing with sensors and actuators, as well as general I/O. Most boards include a 5-volt linear regulator and a 16 MHz crystal oscillator. An Arduino's microcontroller comes with a boot loader that simplifies uploading of programs to the on-chip flash memory. The Arduino board brings out the microcontroller's I/O pins for use by external circuits.

Boards are programmed over a serial connection. Some Arduino boards contain a simple inverter circuit to convert between RS-232-level and TTL-level signals. Newer Arduino boards are programmed via RS-232 protocol over USB.

The Arduino IDE is a cross-platform application implemented in Java. It is designed to introduce programming to newcomers unfamiliar with traditional software development. It includes a code editor with features such as syntax highlighting, parenthesis matching, automatic indentation, and is also capable of compiling and uploading programs to the board with a single click. There is no need to edit makefiles or run programs on the command line.

The Arduino IDE comes with a C/C++ library called "Wiring", which makes many common input/output operations much easier. It uses the gnu toolchain and AVR libraries. The Atmel Development Studio can also be used. Arduino programs are generally written in a variant of c/c++.

The Arduino hardware reference designs are distributed under an Open Source Creative Commons Attribution Share-Alike 2.5 license and are available on the Arduino Web site. Layout and production files for some versions of the Arduino hardware are also available. The source code for the IDE and the on-board library are available and released under the GPLv2 license.

Intel involvement with ARM

The StrongARM was a family of microprocessors that implemented the ARM V4 instruction set architecture (ISA). It was developed by Digital Equipment Corporation (DEC) and later sold along with the license to Intel, who continued to manufacture it before replacing it with their Xscale series.

Intel had discontinued the SA-1110 in early 2003. The SA-1110 was available in 133 or 206 MHz versions. It differed from the SA-1100 by featuring support for 133 MHz 206 MHz. Synchronous dynamic random access memory (SDRAM) was supported. Its companion chip, which provided additional support for peripherals, was the SA-1111. It was used in mobile phones, and personal data assistants (PDAs).

The X-Scale microprocessor core is Intel's and Marvell's implementation of the ARMv5 architecture, and consists of several distinct families. The XScale Application Processors include the I/O Processors (IOP); the Network Processors (IXP); the Control Plane Processors (IXC); and the Consumer Electronics Processors (CE). The XScale effort at Intel was started after the purchase of DEC's StrongARM division in 1998.

In June 2006, Intel sold the XScale PXA business to Marvell Technology Group. This allowed Intel to focus its resources on its core x86 architecture and server businesses. Intel continues manufacturing XScale processors for Marvell. Intel continues to hold an ARM license as well.

Compare and Contrast, Intel embedded versus ARM

Intel has traditionally made embedded processors based on its general purpose line. ARM, on the other hand, targeted the Embedded world specifically, although some general purpose products have emerged. The ARM processors have always been designed for low power usage. Intel focuses on the high performance desktops and servers, where ARM dominates the embedded market. Intel's X-86 architecture is CISC, the ARM is a RISC architecture. With CISC, there are variable length instructions. RISC uses standard instruction lengths for optimizing use of the execution pipeline. The latest Intel ATOM processors, found on the desk, in laptops, and in embedded, have similar thermal performance to ARM.

All ARM instructions can be conditionally executed. In the x86, only the MOV instruction can. With its variable-length instructions, the x86 doesn't worry about instruction alignment in memory. Arm has vector floating point, and Neon, for DSP operastions. Intel has SSE. On Intel, if a division by zero is accidentally executed, it is fatal to the running program. In the ARM architecture, this causes a hardware trap, and a trap handler can flag the error state. In ARM and x86 parameters are passed on the stack, or in registers. X86 is little-endian, and ARM can be either.

ARM Holdings PLC, a British Multinational company, is the owner of the intellectual property (IP) of the CPU design, and licenses its use worldwide. It does not produce chips. Intel is both a design house, with the proprietary x86 architecture, and a fabrication facility. Intel holds a license to produce ARM architecture chips.

Both ARM and Intel support out-of-order execution. Each have SIMD, single instruction, multiple data, or vector processing, the Intel SSE/MMX, and the ARM NEON. Both have implemented single and double precision IEEE floating point.

The boot process differs between the x86 and the ARM. In the Intel architecture, upon power-up the CPU is operating in real mode, and acceses address FFFF:0000 and begins executing there. Since this is only 16 bytes, what is normally there is a long jump to the location of the initialization code and bootloader, which is termed the BIOS. The BIOS can be in ROM, or in flash. The bootloader operates in real, not protected, mode, because the memory has not been set up yet. In ARM, the process is similar. At power-on-reset, the processor jumps to location 0 in low memory, and finds a jump instruction to This might be in flash, or in rom. Later ARM architectures support the high vector, at the top of memory. This is set by a input signal.

We don't want to run from flash, so one of the bootloader's initialization tasks is to load the operating system code to ram, from flash, a hard drive, or

37

whatever secondary storage we have.

STM-32

STMicroelectronics manufactures the STM32F line of 32-bit ARM Cortex models for embedded applications. These are embedded computers, including CPU, memory, and I/O. There are 100's of variants with different performance and peripherals to address a broad spectrum of applications. They have three main families, high performance, mainstream, and low power. STM also manufacturers an 8-bit MCU.

The STM 32F103 is a typical 32-bit MCU in the ARM Cortex line. It has the M3 core, and runs at a maximum frequency of 72 MHz. It includes 20 kbytes of SRAM, and up to 128 kbytes of flash memory. The SRAM operates at the CPU clock speed. It has power-on reset, which loads the program counter with the value in the reset vector which is at memory address 4. A 32 KHz oscillator is included for the real-time clock. The clock maintains time and date, and can provide an alarm interrupt or periodic interrupt. Three low power modes are implemented: sleep, stop, and standby. In sleep mode, the cpu clock is stopped but the peripherals are awake, and can awaken the CPU. Stop mode has all of clocks stopped. Content of the SRAM and registers are maintained. The chip can be awakened with the EXTI line, a non-maskable external interrupt. Standby mode has the lowest power consumption. Memory and register contents are lost. Standby mode is exited with a WKUP external signal or a NRST. The real time clock can also force an exit from Standby; its clock is not stopped in that mode.

The chip includes dual 12-bit analog to digital converters, with up to 16 channels available by multiplexing. There are seven channels of DMA available, timers, USARTS, and SPI and I2C support on I/O channels. There are a maximum of 80 map-able I/O ports that can be configured, and 16 vectored external interrupts. At reset, the vector table is at address 0. The chip runs on 3.3 volts, but the inputs are 5 volt tolerant. A JTAG debugging port is available. There are three 16-bit timers that can be used for quadrature encoder input, or PWM output, and two watchdog timers. The 16-bit general purpose timers can count up or down, and have a capture/compare feature. The watchdog timer is independent of the main clock.

Standard communication interfaces that are supported include I^2C, USART, SPI (at 18 mbps), CAN, and USB 2.0. One or two I2C buses can be supported in multi-master or slave modes. The USART interface operates up to 4.5 Mbps, and can use DMA. The SPI interface can operate to 18 Mbps in full duplex and master mode. Can bus supports 2.0A and B formats to 1 Mbps, and uses frames with 11- or 29-bit identifiers. The USB interface goes to 12 Mbps. The chip includes a CRC calculation circuit with a 96-bit capacity. The STM32F represents a family chips, with low-, medium-, and high density models. Higher density models include more memory and I/O devices. The chip can be configured to boot from system memory, user flash, or internal SRAM.

Any of the general purpose I/O pins can be software configured to be an input or an output. The two built-in analog-digital converters share 16 channels, and include sample and hold. The chip also has an internal temperature sensor with a voltage that varies linearly with temperature. This is connected internally to ADC channel 12, input 16.

Compare and Contrast Quark with STM32F1

Parameter	Quark	STM32F1
CPU	32bit	32 bit
Architecture	x86	ARM Cortex M3
ISA	x86	ARM Cortex- M
Icache	8k, 2-way	n/a
DSP	ARCv2	n/a
Pattern match	128 neurons	n/a
Flash	384k	64 or 128k
OTP	8k, 2-way	n/a
Ram	80k	20k
timers	4	7
watchdog	1	2
RTC	1	1
UART	2	yes
SPI	2	yes
GPIO	32+16	80
USB	1	yes
I2C	2+2	yes
I2S	2	yes
ADC	19 x 12-bit	varies
analog compare	19	n/a

DMA	8	7
security	OTP	n/a
security	JTAGblock	n/a
security	NVM	N/A
pins	144	144
states	3	4

Intel x-86 Embedded

This section discusses the x-86 embedded architecture, built around the x86 Atom processor, with added features for the embedded environment. This takes the form of included memory and I/O, so we can have a single chip solution.

Intel Quark

The Intel Quark SE is a 32-bit x86 architecture SOC. The cpu operates at 32 MHz. It does not support floating point operations, but does have an 8-kbyte instruction cache. The sensor subsystem includes a 32-bit Argonaut DSP-RISC core which does support floating point, and a hardware-based pattern matching accelerator, with 128 "neurons." There is 384 kbytes of flash memory, and 80 kbytes of SRAM, which is shared between the processors. There are 5 timers, one of which is the watchdog. For I/O, it supports dual UART's, dual SPI, usb, 32 GPIO's, and 2 general purpose i^2c's and 2 master-only i^2c's in the sensor section. The are also dual i2s and 19 analog comparators (no A/D). The system has 8 dma channels. All of this is on a 10mm x 10mm package.

The Argonaut RISC (ARC) Core refers to a 32-bit architecture by ARC International. They use a specific ISA that the company developed for high speed execution along with low power. These are the Synopsys processor family, optimized for energy and performance. The user code and Arduino libraries run on the ARC Core, which is neither an x85 nor ARM architecture.

The Zephyr small-footprint Open Source Kernel OS runs on the Quark processor core. It is a project of the linux foundation, that Intel contributed to.

The architecture also has the XD (execute disabled) bit for security. This allows memory pages to be marked as data-only. This counters software exploits and buffer-overflow attacks.

The Intel Galileo board was based on the Quark SoC X1000, and was the first Intel board that was hardware and software compatible with the Arduino shields. It is now retired.

Intel Curie

The Intel Curie SOC Module is a 32-bit System-on-a-chip, using the Quark processor. The module can be hosted on a development board, with interfacing connectors. The module was announced in 2015.

The integrated digital signal processor based sensor hub interfaces with the included BOSCH BMI160 6-axis accelerometer/gyro. These devices are interfaced via SPI. There is also a I^2C interface for an external magnetometer. JTAG is supported.

There is a pattern matching engine, that identifies motions and activities, using the 6-axis sensor. It compares these with previously stored values in memory. The device includes a low power Bluetooth module, for wireless interfacing with external devices. The module footprint is 11 x 8 mm in size, and 2 mm tall.

The device comes with a bootloader in flash, that can be re-installed over JTAG.

Intel Edison

The Intel Edison is a SOM that is the basis for the Arduino-101 board, and the Edison Break-out board, which is a little bigger than an Arduino. It has a dual-core, dual-thread 32-bit Atom cpu operating at 500 MHz, and a 32-bit Quark microcontroller operating at 100 MHz. The Edison is also the basis of the somewhat larger IoT Analytics board, which interfaces with aps on the Cloud for data analytics.

Intel Arduino-101

The Arduino-101 from Intel uses the Curie module on an Arduino-compatible board, and is compatible with the Arduino at the source, and, generally, I/O level. This is a x86 architecture, not an ARM. Existing Arduino sketches will run, if recompiled. The product is targeted to the Internet of Things space.

Diligent did a similar thing with their chipKIT Uno32, which used a Microchip PIC processor on a board similar to the Arduino Uno. It was compatible with the

ARM version at the source code level, and with the Arduino world at the hardware level.

The 101 board is supported by the Arduino Desktop IDE, by selecting the -101 in the Boards Manager function. It uses 3.3 volts, and includes Bluetooth, and the six-axis accelerometer and gyro. The board is identical to the Arduino Uno in size and pinout. The Uno uses the Atmega328p ARM CPU.

The -101 board has 14 digital I/O's , and 6 analog inputs. It has a usb for communication with a development host, and supports I2C. Arduino sketches are run on the RISC core by default. Intel provides a Open Developer Kit (ODK) for the Curie.

IoT

The next big idea in deploying embedded systems involves the integration of cheap embedded devices with web services. The Internet of Things refers to smart connected objects, such as small embedded controllers, smart sensors, and smart actuators. We implement uniquely identifiable objects, with an addressing scheme, perhaps a URL.

The very-low-cost, high-performance microprocessor-based embedded systems enable wide usage. The Internet and wireless allow complete distance-insensitive world-wide connectivity. Cloud servers allow access to "unlimited" datasets.

We can have universal world-wide connectivity, using

.net framework, which is free and open source software. Net framework allows the embedded device to be a http client. It can access data, provide data, and access services. It handles the hard part with code for requests and the socket interface., and is off-the-shelf libraries. It is available per-programmed into flash, and provides access to a huge ecosystem. The .net framework supports the popular x86 and Ardunio hardware architecture. There is a specific variant call the Netduino.

So now, not only people with desktops, laptops, tablets and phone can populate the Internet, along with the server/cloud architecture, but devices can as well. This concept of IoT just kicked off around 2014, but has seen tremendous growth. It is estimated that there are more "things" on the internet, than people. These are event driven. There is some concern this whole structure will become non-deterministic, even practically. It's just too complex, and feeding upon itself.

The applications are limited only by imagination. Nodes can be self-organizing. There is already a completely wired smart city in Korea, Songdo. Computers were built into the houses, streets ,and offices as part of a city-wide wide area network

We need to architect and implement the IoT carefully. At least as long as we are in charge. It can provide a whole new world-wide platform for cyber-attacks. How can it be managed? Can it be managed? It is a rapidly evolving system, with positive feedback. There are privacy concerns. Now that this is working, we can't put the Genie back in the bottle. We can only hold on, and hope to steer. Does the Internet of Things need us?

Intel addresses the IoT market with its 12th generation embedded versions of the Xeon D-, W- , Gold, and Silver. Some of these work at 5 Ghz.

Thr Intel Deep Learning (DL) Boost provides built-in acceleration for workloads for training and interface. This includes the AVX-512. This implements 512 bit vector operations. AVX is Advanced Vector Extensions. Intel also has the AI Analytics Toolkit, and the Open VINO toolkit.

Wrap-up

Intel has been in the embedded processor business almost as long as it has been producing embedded processors. It's approach has been to develop embedded versions of its desk-top bound cpu's. Although any general purpose can server as an embedded processor (the first ones were mainframes), a purpose built unit with included memory and I/O is better. Intel is still major player in the desktop/server market, but has set its sights on the volume market of embedded chips. It has set its sights on the de facto hardware standard, the Arduino. With the Curie module on the-101 board, we have an Arduino along with a RISC core that executes the ARM instructions. The x86 architecture has survived the test of time. Intel provides the proper tools and libraries to allow the x86 inside to operate with existing

Arduino interfaces. At the source code level, this all works fine, and Intel has solved the quirky differences that would prevent full compatibility. I, for one, would like to have a 64-bit Arduino with Teraflop capability, and I won't ask too many questions about what's inside the chip. Oh, could I get that Rad-hard?

References

Ganssle, Jack; Noergaard, Tammy; Eady, Fred; and Edwards, Lewin; *Embedded Hardware*, Newnes, 2007, ISBN-978-0750685849.

Ganssle, Jack, *The Art of Designing Embedded Systems* (EDN Series for Design Engineers) Newnes, 1999, ISBN-978-0750698696.

Ganssle, Jack and Barr, Mike *Embedded Systems Dictionary*, CMP; 1st edition, 2003, ISBN- 1578201209.

Ganssle, Jack *The Firmware Handbook*, Newnes; 1st edition, 2004, ISBN- 075067606X.

Hennessy, John L. and Patterson, David A. *Computer Architecture, Fifth Edition: A Quantitative Approach*, Morgan Kaufmann,, 2011, ISBN 012383872X.

Intel, Embedded Controller Handbook, (80186, 80188), 1987, 210918, ISBN 1555121217.

Intel Microprocessor and Peripheral Handbook, 2 Vol., 1987, 230843.

Seal, David ARM *Architecture Reference Manual,* 2nd Edition, 2001 Addison Wesley, ISBN 0201737191.

Stakem, Patrick H. *4- and 8-bit Microprocessors, Architecture and History*, 2013, PRRB Publishing, ASIN B00D5ZSKCC.

Stakem, Patrick H. *16-bit Microprocessors, History and Architecture*, 2013 PRRB Publishing, ASIN B00D5ETQ3U.

Stakem, Patrick H. *Computer Architecture & Programming of the Intel x86 Family*; 2012, PRRB Publishing, ASIN: B0078Q39D4.

Stakem, Patrick H. *Embedded Computer Systems, Volume 1, Introduction and Architecture,* 2013, PRRB Publishing, ASIN B00GB0W4GG, ASIN B00GB0W4GG.

Stakem, Patrick H. *The Architecture and Applications of the ARM Microprocessors, a Resource Guide*, 2nd ed, 2014, PRRB Publishing, ASIN B00BAFF4OQ,

Stakem, Patrick H. *Floating Point Computation*, 2013, PRRB Publishing, ASIN B00D5E1S7W.

Stakem, Patrick H. *Architecture of Massively Parallel Microprocessor Systems*, 2011, PRRB Publishing, ASIN B004K1F172.

Stakem, Patrick H. *Multicore Computer Architecture,* 2014, PRRB Publishing, ASIN B00KB2XIQD.
Stakem, Patrick H. *RISC Microprocessors, History and Overview,* 2013, PRRB Publishing, ASIN B00D5SCHQO.

Stakem, Patrick H. *Mainframes, Computing on Big Iron*, 2015, PRRB Publishing, ASIN B00TXQQ3FI.

Stakem, Patrick H. *Virtualization and the Cloud,* 3rd ed, 2016, PRRB Publishing, ASIN B00BAFF0JA.

Wolf, Wayne, *High-Performance Embedded Computing: Architectures, Applications, and Methodologies, Morgan Kaufmann, 2006, ISBN- 978-0123694850.*

Wolf, Marilyn, *High-Performance Embedded Computing: Applications in Cyber-Physical Systems and Mobile Computing,* 2nd Edition, 2014, Morgan Kaufmann, ISBN-978-0124105119.

wikipedia, various. Material from Wikipedia (www.wikipedia.org) is used under the conditions of the Creative commons Attribution-ShareAlike #.0 Unported License.
http://creativecommons.org/licenses/by-sa/3,0

Resources

http://www.st.com/en/microcontrollers.html
  (STM)

https://software.intel.com/en-us/node/675551
  (Curie)

http://www.intel.com/content/www/us/en/company-overview/intel-museum.html (Intel)

ARC ISA see,
me.bios.io/images/d/dd/ARCompactISA_Programmers Reference.pdf

Intel Atom

www.intel.com/content/.../atom-e3800-graphics-media-performance-white-paper.pdf

www.intel.com/.../image-processing-opening-new-possibilities-ip-cameras-brief.pdf

www.intel.com/content/.../intelligent.../core-image-signal-processing-presentation.htm.

www.intel.com/content/dam/www/.../atom-processor-e3900-series-product-brief.pdf

www.nasoftware.co.uk/home/attachments/019_Atom_benchmarks.pdf

Matassa, Lon; Domeika, Max, *Break Away with Intel*

Atom Processors: A Guide to Architecture Migration, Intel Press, 2010, ISBN-1934053376.

4004/4040

Myslewski, Rik *Happy 40th Birthday Intel 4004*, The Register, December 15, 2011, Amazon Digital Services, Inc.. ASIN: B006MSQKOE.

Busicom 141-PF calculator and the Intel 4004 microprocessor,

http://www.vintagecalculators.com/html/busicom_141-pf_and_intel_4004.html

http://www.intel4004.com

http://www.intel.com/Assets/PDF/DataSheet/4004_datasheet.pdf

8008/8080/8085

Cohn, David L. *A Step by Step Introduction to 8080 Microprocessor Systems,* Dilithium Press, 1977, ISBN-0918398045.

Maples, Michael D. *Floating Point Package for Intel 8008 and 8080 Microprocessors,* Oct. 24, 1975, Lawrence Livermore Lab, University of California.

Intel, Embedded Controller Handbook, (80186, 80188), 1987, Intel 210918.

Intel Microprocessor and Peripheral Handbook, 2 Vol., 1987, Intel 230843.

Kumar, N. Sentil Saravanan, M. and Jeevananthan, S. Microprocessors and Microcontrollers Oxford University Press, USA, 2011, ISBN-10: 0198066473.

Lalond, David *The 8080, 8085, and Z80: Hardware, Software, Programming, Interfacing, and Troubleshooting*, Prentice Hall, 1988,ISBN-013247008X.

Larsen, David G. *8080/8085 Software Design*, Howard W Sams, 1st ed., 1979, ISBN- 0672215411.

Osborne, Adam *8080 Programming for Logic Design*, 1976, Sybex, ASIN B00073F4JW.

Phillips, George M. *The Collector's Guide to Vintage Intel Microchips,* 2006, (CD-ROM), Smithsonian, ISBN 0977239608.

Rony, Peter R. T*he 8080A Bugbook: Microcomputer Interfacing and Programming*, 1977, Sams, ISBN 0672214474.

Uffenbeck, John *Microcomputers and Microprocessors: The 8080, 8085, and Z-80 Programming, Interfacing, and Troubleshooting* (3rd Edition), 1999, Prentice Hall, ISBN 0132091984.

The 8080/8085 Microprocessor Book, Intel Corp. 1980, Wiley, ISBN-0471035688.

Intel 8051

Intel 8 bit Embedded Control Handbook, Jan. 92, ISBN-1555121217.

Ayala, Kenneth J. *The 8051 Microcontroller.* 3rd ed. Clifton Park, NY: Thomson Delmar Learning, 2004, ISBN-10: 140186158X.

Ayala, Kenneth J. *8051 Microprocessor: Architecture, Programming, and Applications,* 1997, West Publishing Co. ISBN- 0314772782.

Caqlcutt, David et al, *8051 Microcontroller: An Applications Based Introduction,* 1st ed, Newnes, 2004, ISBN-0750657596

Karakehayov, Zdravko, Knud Smed Christensen, and Ole Winther. *Embedded systems design with 8051 microcontrollers : Hardware and software.* Electrical Engineering and Electronics. Vol. 108. 1999, New York: Marcel Dekker.

Mazide, Muhammad Ali, *The 8051 Microcontroller and Embedded Systems,* 2nd ed, Pearson, 2005, ISBN-013119402X,

Predko, Mike *Programming and Customizing the 8051 Microcontroller,* New York: McGraw-Hill/Tab, 1999, ISBN- 0071341927.

Intel i960

i960 Processors and Related Products, Intel Corp., 1994,

ISBN-1555122345.

Myers, Glenford J. and Budde, David L. The 80960 Microprocessor Architecture, 1988, Wiley-Interscience, 1st ed, ISBN-0471618578.

Intel Edison

Moyerman, Stephanie, *Getting Started with Intel Edison: Sensors, Actuators, Bluetooth, and Wi-Fi on the Tiny Atom-Powered Linux Module,* Maker Media, Inc., 1st ed, 2015, ISBN-1457187590 .

Fairhead, Harry *Explore Intel Edison*, I/O Press, 2016, ISBN-1871962447.

Kurniawan, Agus, *The Hands-on Intel Edison Manual Lab*, 1st ed, 2014, ASIN – B00QOXR0JG.

Norris, Donald *Programming the Intel Edison: Getting Started with Processing and Python* ,1st Edition, 2015, McGraw-Hill Education TAB, ASIN-B0155RT21A .

Intel Quark

Richardson, Matt Getting Started with Intel Galileo, 1st ed, 2014, Maker Media, Inc. ASIN- B00J0HH016.

MMX

Intel Architecture MMX ™ Technology: Programmers Reference Manual, Intel Corp, 1996, ASIN-B000EZIDAK .

Using Intel Streaming SIMD extensions and Intel Integrated Performance Primitives to Accelerate Algorithms, 2016, avail: https://software.intel.com/en-us/articles/using-intel-streaming-simd-extensions-and-intel-integrated-performance-primitives-to-accelerate-algorithms.

IoT

Greengard, Samuel *The Internet of Things*, MIT Press, 2015, ASIN-B00VB7I9VS.

Jaokar, Ajit Vijaykumar, *Data Science for Internet of Things,2015,* ISBN-1518819710.

Nagpure, Amin *IOT Enabled: Internet of Things Enabled, Includes Sample Project using Nodejs with Arduino Uno Board,* 2016, Amazon Digital Services, ASIN-B01GAAV4OY.

Glossary

1's complement – a binary number representation scheme for negative values.

2's complement – another binary number representation scheme for negative values.

Accumulator – a register to hold numeric values during and after an operation.

ACM – Association for Computing Machinery; professional organization.

ACPI – Advanced Configuration and Power Interface, Industry Standard.

A/D, ADC – analog to digital converter

ALU – arithmetic logic unit.

AMP – asymmetric multiprocessing.

Android – an operating system based on Gnu-Linux, popular for smart phones and tablet computers.

Analog – concerned with continuous values.

ANSI – American National Standards Institute

API – application program interface; specification for software modules to communicate.

Arduino – open source, single board microcontroller using an Atmel AVR (8-bit risc) cpu.

ARC – Argonaut RISC Core, by ARC International.

ARM – Acorn RISC machine; a 32-bit architecture with wide application in embedded systems.

ASIC – application specific integrated circuit, custom or

semicustom,.

Assembly language – low level programming language specific to a particular ISA.

Async – asynchronous; using different clocks.

AVR – a family of microcontrollers from Atmel.

Baud – symbol rate; may or may not be the same as bit rate.

BCD – binary coded decimal. 4-bit entity used to represent 10 different decimal digits; with 6 spare states.

Beowulf – clustering technology for Gnu-Linux-based computers.

Big-endian – data format with the most significant bit or byte at the lowest address, or transmitted first.

Binary – using base 2 arithmetic for number representation.

BIOS – basic input output system; first software run after boot.

BIST – built-in self test.

Bit – smallest unit of digital information; two states.

Bluetooth – short range radio link between systems.

Boolean – a data type with two values; an operation on these data types; named after George Boole, mid-19th century inventor of Boolean algebra.

Bootstrap – a startup or reset process that proceeds without external intervention.

BSD – Berkeley Software Distribution version of the

Bell Labs Unix operating system.

BSP – board support package; information and drivers for a specific circuit board.

Buffer – a temporary holding location for data.

Bug – an error in a program or device.

Bus – data channel, communication pathway for data transfer.

Byte – ordered collection of 8 bits; values from 0-255

C – programming language from Bell Labs, circa 1972.

Cache – faster and smaller intermediate memory between the processor and main memory.

Cache coherency – process to keep the contents of multiple caches consistent.

CAN – Controller Area Network, a proprietary bus from Siemens.

Chip – integrated circuit component.

CISC – complex instruction set computer.

Clock – periodic timing signal to control and synchronize operations.

CMOS – complementary metal oxide semiconductor; a technology using both positive and negative semiconductors to achieve low power operation.

Complement – in binary logic, the opposite state.

Compilation – software process to translate source code to assembly or machine code (or error codes).

Configware – equivalent of software for FPGA architectures; configuration information.

Control Flow – computer architecture involving directed flow through the program; data dependent paths are allowed.

COP – computer operating properly.

Coprocessor – another processor to supplement the operations of the main processor. Used for floating point, video, etc. Usually relies on the main processor for instruction fetch; and control.

Core – early non-volatile memory technology based on ferromagnetic toroid's.

Cots – commercial, off-the-shelf.

CPU – central processing unit.

CRC – cyclic redundancy code.

D/A – digital to analog conversion.

DAC – digital to analog converter.

Dataflow – computer architecture where a changing value forces recalculation of dependent values.

DDR – dual data rate (memory).

Deadlock – a situation in which two or more competing actions are each waiting for the other to finish, and thus neither ever does.

Denorm – in floating point representation, a non-zero number with a magnitude less than the smallest normal number.

Device driver – specific software to interface a peripheral to the operating system.

Digital – using discrete values for representation of

states or numbers.

Dirty bit – used to signal that the contents of a cache have changed.

DMA - direct memory access (to/from memory, for I/O devices).

Double word – two words; if word = 8 bits, double word = 16 bits.

DRAM – dynamic random access memory.

DSP – digital signal processing.

EIA – Electronics Industry Association.

Embedded system – a computer systems with limited human interfaces and performing specific tasks.

Eprom – erasable programmable read-only memory.

EEprom – electrically erasable read-only memory.

Ethernet – 1980's networking technology. IEEE 802.3.

Exception – interrupt due to internal events, such as overflow.

Fetch/execute cycle – basic operating cycle of a computer; fetch the instruction, execute the instruction.

FIFO – first in, first out.

Firmware – code contained in a non-volatile memory.

Fixed point – computer numeric format with a fixed number of digits or bits, and a fixed radix point. Integers.

Flag – a binary state variable.

Flash memory – a type of non-volatile memory, similar to EEprom.

Flip-flop – a circuit with two stable states; ideal for binary.

Floating point – computer numeric format for real numbers; has significant digits and an exponent.

FPGA – field programmable gate array.

FPU – floating point unit, an ALU for floating point numbers.

Full duplex – communication in both directions simultaneously.

Gate – a circuit to implement a logic function; can have multiple inputs, but a single output.

Giga - 10^9 or 2^{30}

Gnu – recursive acronym; gnu (is) not unix. Operating system that is free & open source software.

GPIO – general purpose Input-Output. Usually referred to a single digital line.

GPL – gnu public license used for free software; referred to as the "copyleft."

GPU – graphics processing unit. ALU for graphics data.

GUI – graphics user interface.

Half-duplex – communications in two directions, but not simultaneously.

Handshake – co-ordination mechanism.

Harvard architecture – memory storage scheme with separate instructions and data.

Hexadecimal – base 16 number representation.

Hexadecimal point – radix point that separates integer from fractional values of hexadecimal numbers.

HSS – high speed serial.

Hypervisor – virtual machine manager. Can manage multiple operating systems.

I^2C – inter-integrated circuit; a multi-master serial single-ended computer bus invented by Philips.

I^2S - Integrated Inter-IC Sound Bus, serial interface

IA-32 - Intel's instruction set architecture, 32 bit.

IA-64 - Intel's instruction set architecture, 64 bit.

IDE – Integrated development environment for software or configware.

IEEE – Institute of Electrical and Electronic Engineers. Professional organization and standards body.

IEEE-754 – standard for floating point representation and operations.

Infinity - the largest number that can be represented in the number system.

Integer – the natural numbers, zero, and the negatives of the natural numbers.

Interrupt – an asynchronous event to signal a need for attention (example: the phone rings).

Interrupt vector – entry in a table pointing to an interrupt service routine; indexed by interrupt number.

I/O – Input-output from the computer to external devices, or a user interface.

IoT - Internet of Things

IP – intellectual property; also internet protocol.

IP core – IP describing a chip design that can be licensed to be instantiated in an FPGA or ASIC.

IPP – Intel Integrated Performance Prinitives.

ISA – instruction set architecture, the software description of the computer.

ISO – International Standards Organization.

ISR – interrupt service routine, a subroutine that handles a particular interrupt event.

JTAG – Joint Test Action Group; responsible for IEEE 1149.1, Standard Test Access Port and Boundary-Scan Architecture.

JVM – Java Virtual Machine – software that allows any architecture to execute Java bytecodes by emulation.

Kernel – main portion of the operating system. Interface between the applications and the hardware.

Kilo – a prefix for 10^3 or 2^{10}

LAN – local area network.

Linux – unix-like operating system developed by Linus Torvalds; open source.

List – a data structure.

Little-endian – data format with the least significant bit or byte at the highest address, or transmitted last.

Logic operation – generally, negate, AND, OR, XOR, and their inverses.

Loop-unrolling – optimization of a loop for speed at the cost of space.

LPC – low pin count.

LRU – least recently used; an algorithm for item replacement in a cache.

LSB – least significant bit or byte.

LUT – look up table.

Machine language – native code for a particular computer hardware.

Mainframe – a computer you can't lift.

Mantissa – significant digits (as opposed to the exponent) of a floating point value.

Master-slave – control process with one element in charge. Master status may be exchanged among elements.

Math operation – generally, add, subtract, multiply, divide.

MCU – microcontroller unit.

Mega - 10^6 or 2^{20}

Memory leak – when a program uses memory resources but does not return them, leading to a lack of space.

Mesh – a highly connected network.

MESI – modified, exclusive, shared, invalid state of a cache coherency protocol.

Metaprogramming – programs that produce or modify other programs.

Mhz – million (10^6) hertz.

Microcode – hardware level data structures to translate machine instructions into sequences of circuit level operations.

Microcontroller – microprocessor with included memory and/or I/O.

Microprocessor – a monolithic cpu on a chip.

MIMD – multiple instruction, multiple data

Minicomputer – smaller than a mainframe, larger than a pc.

MIPI-CSI - Mobile Industry Processor Interface (Alliance) Camera Serial Interface.

MIPS – millions of instructions per second; sometimes used as a measure of throughput.

mm – millimeter.

MMU – memory management unit; translates virtual to physical addresses.

MMX – Intel multi media extensions, new instructions.

MpSoc – Multi Processor System on a chip.

MPU – memory protection unit.

MSB – most significant bit or byte.

Multiplex – combining signals on a communication channel by sampling.

Mutex – a data structure and methodology for mutual exclusion.

Multicore – multiple processing cores on one substrate or chip; need not be identical.

NAN – not-a-number; invalid bit pattern.

NAND – negated (or inverse) AND function.

NDA – non-disclosure agreement; legal agreement protecting IP.

NEON – advanced SIMD support in ARM architecture.

Nibble – 4 bits, ½ byte.

NIST – National Institute of Standards and Technology (US), previously, National Bureau of Standards.

NMI – non-maskable interrupt; cannot be ignored by the software.

NOR – negated (or inverse) OR function

Normalized number – in the proper format for floating point representation.

NUMA – non-uniform memory access for multiprocessors; local and global memory access protocol.

NVM – non-volatile memory.

OBD – On-Board diagnostics; for automobiles, a state-of-health systems for emissions control.

OCD – on-chip debug.

ODK – Open Developer Kit (Intel).

Off-the-shelf – commercially available; not custom.

Opcode – part of a machine language instruction that specifies the operation to be performed.

Open source – methodology for hardware or software development with free distribution and access.

OS - Operating system ,software that controls the allocation of resources in a computer.

OTP – one-time programmable.

Overflow - the result of an arithmetic operation exceeds the capacity of the destination.

Packet – a small container; a block of data on a network.

Paging – memory management technique using fixed size memory blocks.

Paradigm – a pattern or model

Paradigm shift – a change from one paradigm to another. Can be disruptive or evolutionary.

Parallel – multiple operations or communication proceeding simultaneously.

Parity – an error detecting mechanism involving an extra check bit in the word.

PC – personal computer, politically correct, program counter.

PCB – printed circuit board.

PCI – peripheral interconnect interface (bus).

PCM – pulse code modulation.

Pinout – mapping of signals to I/O pins of a device.

Pipeline – operations in serial, assembly-line fashion.

Pixel – picture element; smallest addressable element on a display or a sensor.

PMOS – positive metal oxide semiconductor.

Posix – portable operating system interface, IEEE

standard.

PROM – programmable read-only memory.

PWM – pulse width modulation.

Quad word – four words. If word = 16 bits, quad word is 64 bits.

Queue – first in, first out data buffer structure; instantiated in hardware of software.

Radix point – separates integer and fractional parts of a real number.

RAM – random access memory; any item can be accessed in the same time as any other.

RAS – Row address strobe, in dram refresh.

Real-time – system that responds to events in a predictable, bounded time.

Register – temporary storage location for a data item.

Reset – signal and process that returns the hardware to a known, defined state.

RISC – reduced instruction set computer.

ROM – read only memory.

Router – networking component for packets.

RTC – real-time clock.

SAM – sequential access memory, like a magnetic tape.

SATA – serial ATA, a storage media interconnect.

Sandbox – an isolated and controlled environment to run untested or potentially malicious code.

SD – Secure Digital (card).

SDIO – Interface extension to SD card, to connect wifi and Bluetooth.

SDRAM – synchronous dynamic random access memory.

Segmentation – dividing a network or memory into sections.

Semiconductor – material with electrical characteristics between conductors and insulators; basis of current technology processor and memory devices.

Semaphore –signaling element among processes.

Sensor – a device that converts a physical observable quantity or event to a signal.

Serial – bit by bit.

Server – a computer providing services on a network.

Shift – move one bit position to the left or right in a word.

Sign-magnitude – number representation with a specific sign bit.

Signed number – representation with a value and a numeric sign.

SIMD – single instruction, multiple data.

SMP – symmetric multiprocessing.

SMT – simultaneous multi threading.

SOC – system on a chip.

Software – set of instructions and data to tell a computer what to do.

SOM – system on a module.

SMP – symmetric multiprocessing.

Snoop – monitor packets in a network, or data in a cache.

SoC – System on a Chip.

Soft core - a hardware description language description of a cpu core.

SPI – Serial peripheral interface, short range, synchronous.

SRAM – static random access memory.

SSE – also SSE2, SSE3 - streaming SIMD extensions (to the x86 instruction set).

SSSE – Supplemental streaming SIMD extension, -3 and -4.

Stack – first in, last out data structure. Can be hardware or software.

Stack pointer – a reference pointer to the top of the stack.

State machine – model of sequential processes.

Superscalar – computer with instruction-level parallelism, by replication of resources.

Synchronous – using the same clock to coordinate operations.

System – a collection of interacting elements and relationships with a specific behavior.

System of Systems – a complex collection of systems with pooled resources.

Table – data structure. Can be multi-dimensional.

Tera - 10^{12} or 2^{40}

Test-and-set – coordination mechanism for multiple processes that allows reading to a location and writing it in a non-interruptible manner.

TCP/IP – transmission control protocol/internet protocol; layered set of protocols for networks.

Thread – smallest independent set of instructions managed by a multiprocessing operating system.

TLB – translation lookaside buffer – a cache of addresses.

TMR – Triple Modular Redundancy; an error control mechanism using redundant components.

Toolchain – set of software tools for development.

Transceiver – receiver and transmitter in one box.

TRAP – exception or fault handling mechanism in a computer; an operating system component.

Tree – files arranged in a tree structure.

Triplicate – using three copies (of hardware, software, messaging, power supplies, etc.). for redundancy and error control.

Truncate – discard. cutoff, make shorter.

TSX-ni – Transactional Synchronization Extensions, Intel X86.

TTL – transistor-transistor logic in digital integrated circuits. (1963)

UART – universal asynchronous receiver-transmitter.

Parallel-to-serial, serial-to-parallel device with handshaking.

Ubuntu – Gnu-Linux variant.

USART – universal synchronous (or) asynchronous receiver/transmitter.

Underflow – the result of an arithmetic operation is smaller than the smallest representable number..

USB – universal serial bus.

Unsigned number – a number without a numeric sign.

Vector – single dimensional array of values.

Virtual memory – memory management technique using address translation.

Virtualization – creating a virtual resource from available physical resources.

VLIW – very long instruction word – mechanism for parallelism.

von Neumann – John, a computer pioneer and mathematician; realized that computer instructions are data.

VPF - (ARM) Vector floating point.

Watchdog – hardware/software function to sanity check the hardware, software, and process; applies corrective action if a fault is detected; fail-safe mechanism.

Wiki – the Hawaiian word for "quick." Refers to a collaborative content website.

WiFi – short range radio-based networking.

Word – a collection of bits of any size; does not have to be a power of two.

Write-back – cache organization where the data is not written to main memory until the cache location is needed for re-use.

Write-through – all cache writes also go to memory.

X86 – Intel -16, -32, 64-bit ISA.

X87 – Intel floating point.

XD – execute disable, an Intel security feature.

XMM – Intel SIMD registers, 128 bit.

XOR – exclusive OR; either but not both.

Zero address – architecture using implicit addressing, like a stack.

If you enjoyed this book, you might also be interested in some of these.

16-bit Microprocessors, History and Architecture, 2013 PRRB Publishing, ISBN-1520210922.

4- and 8-bit Microprocessors, Architecture and History, 2013, PRRB Publishing, ISBN-152021572X,

Apollo's Computers, 2014, PRRB Publishing, ISBN-1520215800.

The Architecture and Applications of the ARM Microprocessors, 2013, PRRB Publishing, ISBN-1520215843.

Earth Rovers: for Exploration and Environmental Monitoring, 2014, PRRB Publishing, ISBN-152021586X.

Embedded Computer Systems, Volume 1, Introduction and Architecture, 2013, PRRB Publishing, ISBN-1520215959.

The History of Spacecraft Computers from the V-2 to the Space Station, 2013, PRRB Publishing, ISBN-1520216181.

Floating Point Computation, 2013, PRRB Publishing, ISBN-152021619X.

Architecture of Massively Parallel Microprocessor Systems, 2011, PRRB Publishing, ISBN-1520250061.

Multicore Computer Architecture, 2014, PRRB Publishing, ISBN-1520241372.

Personal Robots, 2014, PRRB Publishing, ISBN-1520216254.

RISC Microprocessors, History and Overview, 2013, PRRB Publishing, ISBN-1520216289.

Robots and Telerobots in Space Applications, 2011, PRRB Publishing, ISBN-1520210361.

The Saturn Rocket and the Pegasus Missions, 1965, 2013, PRRB Publishing, ISBN-1520209916.

Visiting the NASA Centers, and Locations of Historic Rockets & Spacecraft, 2017, PRRB Publishing, ISBN-1549651205.

Microprocessors in Space, 2011, PRRB Publishing, ISBN-1520216343.

Computer *Virtualization and the Cloud,* 2013, PRRB Publishing, ISBN-152021636X.

What's the Worst That Could Happen? Bad Assumptions, Ignorance, Failures and Screw-ups in Engineering Projects, 2014, PRRB Publishing, ISBN-1520207166.

Computer Architecture & Programming of the Intel x86 Family, 2013, PRRB Publishing, ISBN-1520263724.

The Hardware and Software Architecture of the Transputer, 2011,PRRB Publishing, ISBN-152020681X.

Mainframes, Computing on Big Iron, 2015, PRRB Publishing, ISBN- 1520216459.

Spacecraft Control Centers, 2015, PRRB Publishing, ISBN-1520200617.

Embedded in Space, 2015, PRRB Publishing, ISBN-1520215916.

A Practitioner's Guide to RISC Microprocessor Architecture, Wiley-Interscience, 1996, ISBN-0471130184.

Cubesat Engineering, PRRB Publishing, 2017, ISBN-1520754019.

Cubesat Operations, PRRB Publishing, 2017, ISBN-152076717X.

Interplanetary Cubesats, PRRB Publishing, 2017, ISBN-1520766173 .

Cubesat Constellations, Clusters, and Swarms, Stakem, PRRB Publishing, 2017, ISBN-1520767544.

Graphics Processing Units, an overview, 2017, PRRB Publishing, ISBN-1520879695.

Intel Embedded and the Arduino-101, 2017, PRRB Publishing, ISBN-1520879296.

Orbital Debris, the problem and the mitigation, 2018, PRRB Publishing, ISBN-*1980466483.*

Manufacturing in Space, 2018, PRRB Publishing, ISBN-1977076041.

NASA's Ships and Planes, 2018, PRRB Publishing, ISBN-1977076823.

Space Tourism, 2018, PRRB Publishing, ISBN-1977073506.

STEM – Data Storage and Communications, 2018, PRRB Publishing, ISBN-1977073115.

In-Space Robotic Repair and Servicing, 2018, PRRB Publishing, ISBN-1980478236.

Introducing Weather in the pre-K to 12 Curricula, A Resource Guide for Educators, 2017, PRRB Publishing, ISBN-1980638241.

Introducing Astronomy in the pre-K to 12 Curricula, A Resource Guide for Educators, 2017, PRRB Publishing, ISBN-198104065X.
Also available in a Brazilian Portuguese edition, ISBN-1983106127.

Deep Space Gateways, the Moon and Beyond, 2017, PRRB Publishing, ISBN-1973465701.

Exploration of the Gas Giants, Space Missions to Jupiter, Saturn, Uranus, and Neptune, PRRB Publishing, 2018, ISBN-9781717814500.

Crewed Spacecraft, 2017, PRRB Publishing, ISBN-1549992406.

Rocketplanes to Space, 2017, PRRB Publishing, ISBN-1549992589.

Crewed Space Stations, 2017, PRRB Publishing, ISBN-1549992228.

Enviro-bots for STEM: Using Robotics in the pre-K to 12 Curricula, A Resource Guide for Educators, 2017, PRRB Publishing, ISBN-1549656619.

STEM-Sat, Using Cubesats in the pre-K to 12 Curricula, A Resource Guide for Educators, 2017, ISBN-1549656376.

Embedded GPU's, 2018, PRRB Publishing, ISBN-1980476497.

Mobile Cloud Robotics, 2018, PRRB Publishing, ISBN-1980488088.

Extreme Environment Embedded Systems, 2017, PRRB Publishing, ISBN-1520215967.

What's the Worst, Volume-2, 2018, ISBN-1981005579.

Spaceports, 2018, ISBN-1981022287.

Space Launch Vehicles, 2018, ISBN-1983071773.

Mars, 2018, ISBN-1983116902.

X-86, 40th Anniversary ed, 2018, ISBN-1983189405.

Lunar Orbital Platform-Gateway, 2018, PRRB Publishing, ISBN-1980498628.

Space Weather, 2018, ISBN-1723904023.

STEM-Engineering Process, 2017, ISBN-1983196517.

Space Telescopes, 2018, PRRB Publishing, ISBN-1728728568.

Exoplanets, 2018, PRRB Publishing, ISBN-9781731385055.

Planetary Defense, 2018, PRRB Publishing, ISBN-9781731001207.

Exploration of the Asteroid Belt, 2018, PRRB Publishing, ISBN-1731049846.

Terraforming, 2018, PRRB Publishing, ISBN-1790308100.

Martian Railroad, 2019, PRRB Publishing, ISBN-1794488243.

Exoplanets, 2019, PRRB Publishing, ISBN-1731385056.

Exploiting the Moon, 2019, PRRB Publishing, ISBN-1091057850.

RISC-V, an Open Source Solution for Space Flight Computers, 2019, PRRB Publishing, ISBN-1796434388.

Arm in Space, 2019, PRRB Publishing, ISBN-9781099789137.

Search for *Extraterrestrial Life,* 2019, PRRB Publishing, ISBN-978-1072072188.

Submarine Launched Ballistic Missiles, 2019, ISBN-978-1088954904.

Space Command, Military in Space, 2019, PRRB Publishing, ISBN-978-1693005398.

Robotic Exploration of the Icy moons of the Gas Giants, ISBN- 979-8621431006.

History & Future of Cubesats, ISBN-978-1986536356.

Robotic Exploration of the Icy Moons of the Ice Giants, by Swarms of Cubesats, ISBN-979-8621431006.

Swarm Robotics, ISBN-979-8534505948.

Introduction to Electric Power Systems, ISBN-979-

8519208727.

Powerships, Powerbarges, Floating Wind Farms: electricity when and where you need it, 2021, PRRB Publishing, ISBN-979-8716199477.

Centros de Control: Operaciones en Satélites del Estándar CubeSat (Spanish Edition), 2021, ISBN-979-8510113068.

The Artemis Missions, Return to the Moon, and on to Mars, 2021, ISBN-979-8490532361.

James Webb Space Telescope. A New Era in Astronomy, 2021, ISBN-979-8773857969.